Guangzhou: The History and Legacy of China Center

By Charles River Editors

A Qing-era portrait of the Grotto of the Five Immortals, the Taoist temple around the five stones which gave Guangzhou its nickname "The City of Rams"

About Charles River Editors

Charles River Editors is a boutique digital publishing company, specializing in bringing history back to life with educational and engaging books on a wide range of topics. Keep up to date with our new and free offerings with this 5 second sign up on our weekly mailing list, and visit Our Kindle Author Page to see other recently published Kindle titles.

We make these books for you and always want to know our readers' opinions, so we encourage you to leave reviews and look forward to publishing new and exciting titles each week.

Introduction

Ancient illustrations from the era

The Han Dynasty

The modern day city of Guangzhou is located in the mountainous region of south China. Near the Baiyun Mountains that rise from the edge of the city and the eastern banks of the Pearl River (Zhujiang), the city today covers approximately 7, 400 square kilometers. The location of the city provides it the opportunity to oversee the delta of the Pearl River, which is China's third largest river. This has allowed the city historically and in the present to control the movement of goods into China while the proximity of the city to the South China Sea has allowed merchant ships from around the world to trade goods here.

As a developing and expanding city, the land of Guangzhou has become a valuable commodity that attracts immigrants from regions of Southeast Asia, Europe, western Asia and Africa. Even within China itself, a large number of migrants have moved from other regions of China to Guangzhou making the Chinese migrant population around 30-40% resulting in the city deciding to limit its population growth by 2020 (Guangzhou Population 2018). Most of the residents of the city live in the central districts of the city.

The local language of the people, known as Cantonese, is most commonly referred to as also Cantonese, but is more formally known as Yueyu. Due to the high number of migrants from other regions of China it has become more common to also find Mandarin being spoken. Before the city became a thriving metropolitan area, many people had emigrated to other regions such as Southeast Asia and North America in search of job opportunities. Since the 1980s, populations of Cantonese have begun to return back to the city given the financial success of the region and being one of the best commercial cities on the Chinese mainland (Cheng and Geng 06 April 2017).

The people of the region and the language are known as Cantonese based on the romanization of the name "Guangdong" (the name of the region), which may have been interpreted by the Portuguese as sounding like *Cantão* (Merriam-Webster's 2004: 181). The English then used the term Canton to refer not just to the city, but to the region of Guangdong in general. Since then, the term is used to describe the people, language, culture, and food of the region.

Guangzhou: The History and Legacy of China's Most Influential Trade Center examines how China's third biggest city took shape, from ancient origins to its role in the Silk Road and trade with Europe. Along with pictures depicting important people, places, and events, you will learn about Guangzhou like never before.

Ancient Beginnings

The first peoples of the region were of Tai or Shan origin and settled the region by 1100 B.C. (Short 1992). The first settlement where modern day Guangzhou is located is said to have been Chuting. This establishment was created by the Chu State during the reign of the Zhou Dynasty (1046 to 256 B.C.). By the time of the decline of the Qin Dynasty (221 to 206 B.C.), the city of Panyue, which likely is a transformed version of the earlier Chuting, had already been established. Panyue had become one of the earliest trading ports in China and the eastern most starting point of the Maritime Silk Road. This boom in marketing and trading likely began sometime around the middle of the Tang dynasty (618 to 907 A.D.) (Chin 2004: 217). Products that were being traded from Panyue were mostly of southern origin: ivory, cinnamon, pearl, peacock feathers, rhinoceros horns, and fruit (Müller et al 2004: 8).

During the transition of power from the Qin dynasty to the Han dynasty, the southern kingdom of Nanyue was founded by General Zhao Tuo (reigned 203 to 137 B.C.), and incorporated Panyue as its capital in 204 B.C. Zhao Tuo was a Chinese refugee who moved to the South during the chaotic end days of the Qin dynasty, and killed the Chinese officials that were there. He first declared the independent kingdom of Nanyue (also written Nan Yue) in 207 B.C. The newly formed kingdom incorporated the Guangdong and Guangxi regions as well as Au-lac (present day northern Vietnam) (Walker 2012: 107). Eventually, the Qin dynasty fell and the Han dynasty (206 B.C. to 220 A.D.) rose with Liu Bang as the first emperor.

A later portrait of Liu Bang

The Han dynasty and Nanyue at first formed an uneasy alliance, with Nanyue being considered a vassal state of the Han Empire. The Han Empire had a strong interest in the region, due to its economic and trade potential. Available in the South were important commodities that were not readily available in the north of China. These goods included the trade items mentioned above, but also the abundance of rice that the South could produce. The people of northern China relied on imported rice in order to supplement their diet which consisted mainly of wheat and millet at the time (*ibid*: 108). Zhao Tuo continued to claim independence for his kingdom, and insisted on retaining the title of "Emperor" for his 67 year reign (Twittchet et al 2008). After the death of Zhao Tuo, Zhao Xing attempted to formally join the Nanyue kingdom with the Han Empire. The prime minister, however, disliked the idea and had him killed.

The political instability and coup of the prime minister signaled to the Han Empire that now was an opportune time to expand into the South. Emperor Wu of the Han sent a force of 100,000 men and the region was easily taken, since Nanyue had not been able to establish a significant military during this unstable period (Walker 2012: 109). Nanyue was absorbed into the Han Empire by 111 B.C.

After the incorporation of the Nanyue kingdom into the Han Empire, Panyu became the capital of the region, and trade with the rest of the world continued from Panyue port. The historical recordings of long-distance trade have been confirmed archaeologically through the excavation of numerous Han dynasty tombs. Several tombs from the Nanyue period in the Guangdong region were uncovered between 1955 and 1960 and revealed nineteen clay rhinoceros figures. These particular rhinoceroses were interpreted as being modeled after a type of imported rhinoceros that had been recorded as a tribute to the Chinese court in 2 A.D. Although rhinoceroses could also be found in Southern Asia, there remains the possibility that these were modeled after an imported animal. There is other evidence of the importation of animals from foreign lands that are nevertheless similar to those found in South Asia.

These findings from the Han period suggest a continuation of trade practices established during the Nanyue period. In 1983, archaeologists uncovered the tomb of Zhao Mo, the second king of Nanyue. Inside the tomb were five large pieces of ivory. These ivory pieces were unlike those of the Asian elephant which tends to be narrower and shorter; rather, these ivory pieces were more robust and much longer. This suggests that the ivory was imported to the region, even though ivory would have been available from Asian elephants.

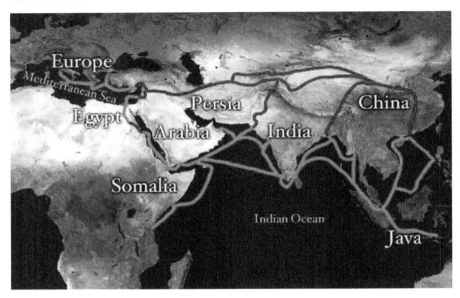

A map of Silk Road routes

The early people of the region, especially the Yue tribes, excelled at shipbuilding and navigation. By the time of the Nanyue kingdom, the region had established its own shipyard. These early ships were not very capable of long-distance maritime voyages, and the early merchants had to rely upon "barbarian junks" in order to travel along the coast. Shipbuilding techniques would improve with the introduction of new methods by Arabic and Persian sailors. By the 8th and 9th centuries A.D. the Chinese junks were sailing the South China Sea and the Indian Ocean conducting trade.

Traders had come from the Middle East to Panyu over the sea by the 7th century A.D., during the Tang dynasty. The Tang dynasty was founded by Li Yuan, a member of the northern aristocratic nobility. Before the founding of the Tang dynasty, the Sui dynasty reigned. It is rumored that the ruler of the Sui dynasty, Yangdi, had heard of a prophecy that foretold the throne would be taken over by a person with the name Li. As such, Yangdi ordered everyone with the name Li to be executed and forced Li Yuan to take action via a rebellion. The rebellion lasted only around a year, and power was transferred to Li Yuan, who would posthumously be given the name Gaozu (Roberts 1999: 50-52).

The traders from the Middle East included the first Muslims to enter China. As with most foreign merchants, these visitors were given racist or derogatory labels such as "Fan," "Wu," "Yi," or "Liao," which generally mean "barbarian" (Jin 1933: 115). This is perhaps partially the result of the city, referred to as *Kuang chou* in some historical records, being sacked by Arabs and Persians in 758 A.D., after which the city was burned, and the assailants returned to the sea (Bretschneider 1871: 10). A couple of years later a vengeful massacre was carried out by Chinese rebels on the wealthy Arab and Persian communities in the northern city of Yangzhou in which 120,000 to 200,000 foreigners were killed. According to Arab histories, another massacre took place in the 9th century at Panyue, with more than 100,000 foreign merchants being targeted and killed (Lewis 2009: 161). Nevertheless, trade continued and the region saw an influx of new cultures and customs that merchants brought with them. The merchants continued to try and settle or assimilate into Chinese Han culture along the waterway regions.

Following the collapse of the Tang dynasty, the Guangdong region became part of the Southern Han, also known as Great Yue and Great Han dynasty (917 to 971 A.D.) with Panyue as its capital. The dynasty was established by Liu Yan who saw himself as a descendant of Liu Bang, founder of the Han dynasty. During this brief period, the region saw great economic success. By this time the influence of foreign concepts of shipbuilding had taken hold, and the Chinese junks were now capable of traveling great distances on their own. No longer did the Chinese merchants need to rely on foreign vessels for their profit.

The long-distance trade routes began with the expansion of the Roman Empire into Egypt in 30 B.C. After the conquest of Egypt, trade routes further east were opened, allowing trade with the Middle East, India, Southeast Asia and China. The Roman Empire absorbed earlier trade routes that had already been established, and began to control them, allowing exports of Roman goods to reach the Far East. The Parthians of Parthia (located in modern day Iran) introduced the Romans to Chinese silk, which started a demand for the material in Europe. So fashionable was the material among the aristocratic women that the Roman senate attempted to ban lower classes from wearing the material. This excessive demand for the material caused a considerable amount of gold to leave the Roman Empire, significantly weakening it by the fifth century A.D.

By this time the Byzantines had discovered the secret of making silk, but quality and craftsmanship were significantly lacking. As such, the demand for Chinese silk continued. Chinese records note the development of this new Byzantine Empire and the embassies that they established during the Tang Dynasty (Halsall 2000). Since the Tang Dynasty invested in the development of long-distance boats, the Chinese vessels could be found in the Persian Gulf, down the Euphrates River in the Middle East, and around the Horn of Africa.

Trade with the West would continue on and off as the empires of the West rose and fell and the dynasties of China changed hands. Over time, the route would be cut off as forces captured key locations along the route such as Tibet. Since the route went from Alexandria, Egypt all the way to Guangzhou, Guangdong, it meant that any conflicts with cultures or empires along these routes would affect the economic and trade systems of all the other regions.

The Silk Road also contributed to the creation of the Mongol Empire in northern China, which would have a significant impact on Chinese history. The Mongol Empire rose to power through trade along the Silk Road, with Genghis Khan establishing capitals of the Empire directly on the route. The Mongols themselves had very little in ways of exports, but would provide merchants with capital and provide protection for them along the Mongol routes. By 1206 A.D., when the Empire first arose, the Mongols had quickly become a formidable force.

Since the beginning of their empire, the Mongols had taken small portions of land from the Chinese, but Chinese ability to rule and remain united was weak. China was divided between the Northern Song dynasty (960 to 1126 A.D.) and Southern Song Dynasty (1127 to 1279 A.D.), with the Northern Song Dynasty suffering a series of wars as various factions competed to establish dynasties. The Jin Dynasty (1115 to 1234 A.D.) was one of the major dynasties to come out from the conflicts in the Northern Song Dynasty region.

When the Jin Dynasty attempted to demand the submission of the Mongol Genghis Khan and to turn his empire into a subservient state in 1210, the Khan refused. In 1211, Genghis declared that the Mongols would go to war against the Jin, and thus began the Mongol-Jin War. The war lasted for roughly 23 years, and the Jin Dynasty received no support from the Southern Song Dynasty. In 1234, the Jin Dynasty was defeated, but the Mongols were not satisfied; they carried out a number of skirmishes with the South Song Dynasty.

A medieval depiction of Genghis Khan

It was not until 1260, under the leadership of the newly elected Kublai Khan, that a full-scale invasion of the Southern Song Dynasty took place. The cost to the Mongols was great, but eventually the invading forces prevailed. In 1271, the Yuan Dynasty (1271-1368 A.D.) was declared, although there would still be many more years of fighting in the region until the Song loyalists were finally defeated. China was once again united, and for the first time ruled by a Mongol Emperor.

Kublai Khan

Guangzhou and the Guangdong region played an important role in the maritime silk route, which was the overseas version of the Silk Road. The route connected China with Southeast Asia, the islands of Indonesia, India, the Arabian peninsula, through Africa to Egypt, and Europe. In 2016, maritime archaeologists discovered a fully laden merchant ship in the South China Sea. The ship dates back to the Southern Song Dynasty (1127 to 1279 A.D.) and is the first attempt by Chinese archaeologists to recover and preserve an ancient merchant vessel. The technical director of the Underwater Cultural Heritage Protection Center of the State Administration of Cultural Heritage, Sun Jian, hopes that this find will help historians and archaeologists understand Chinese navigation techniques, shipbuilding, and life on the overseas maritime trade route (Tao 2016).

By the 14th century, the ethnic Han Chinese had long suffered discrimination by the Mongols over taxation and a series of environmental disasters that led the Chinese to rebel. Rebellions and revolts began breaking out amongst workers in the hundreds of thousands by the 1350s. Zhu Yuanzhang began establishing himself as a leader amongst the rebels and by 1367 had become their undisputed leader. A year later he sent an army into the Yuan capital, Dadu, and founded the Ming dynasty. Dadu was razed to the ground and renamed Beijing.

After the collapse of the Yuan Mongol dynasty, the Great Ming Empire (1368 to 1644 A.D.) was established, and it brought the return of the Han Chinese as rulers of China. The first emperor of the dynasty, Hongwu (Zhu Yuanzhang changed his name for the new era), created a large standing military and one of the largest navy dockyards in the world at the time. Hongwu had declared that trade with foreigners was illegal unless through specific tribute delegations sent by official governments. Around this time, numerous Japanese and Chinese pirates began appearing along the Chinese coast and carried out sporadic raids on settlements in the Guangdong region. The xenophobic attitude towards foreigners and the problem of pirates and illegal trade would be a recurring theme throughout much of the history of Guangdong and Guangzhou until the 20th century.

The Hongwu Emperor

The transition of power from Hongwu to his successor was not a smooth one. Although Hongwu had decided that his grandson Zhu Yunwen should take his place, one of the sons of Hongwu, Zhu Di, disagreed with this appointment. Zhu Di had a good standing in the military and started a civil war with the new emperor who had his name changed to Jianwen for his rule. The revolt of Hongwu was successful after three years of civil war and the standing palace in Nanjing was burned to the ground, along with the royal family, in 1402.

Zhu Di then became the Yongle Emperor and reestablished the Ming Dynasty as he saw fit, which meant reversing many of his father's policies. The recently razed Nanjing was replaced as the capital by Beijing in 1403, and construction of the city lasted until 1420. Another policy of Yongle was the appointment of Zheng He as admiral to a large naval fleet of around 2,000 vessels that had recently been constructed. Yongle had the fleet created so that China could begin a series of tributary missions around the world on an unprecedented scale. The reasoning behind such a tributary fleet was likely a way for the new emperor, who had forced himself upon the throne, to legitimize his rule. The rationalization was that if other countries were recognizing and returning tribute to the emperor's new Ming dynasty, it would make his rule as emperor more legitimate.

The Yongle Emperor

These voyages led by Admiral Zheng He became known as "Xiafan Guanjuan," meaning "foreign expeditionary armada." The first of seven voyages that the fleet took began in 1405. The goal of the voyage was to establish favorable relations with distant lands, and with the fleet came 27,000 troops and goods. The fleet sailed to Champa, Java and all the way to Ceylon and the southern tip of the Indian peninsula before turning back to return to China. The trip was largely seen as a success, and shortly after envoys from the foreign lands the fleet had visited arrived in China bearing tribute and homage.

By the end of the sixth expedition, the Yongle Emperor had died and was succeeded by Zhu Gaozhi, who assumed the name Hongxi as emperor. Hongxi did not view the expeditions favorably and ordered that the fleets cease all diplomatic expeditions. The final voyage would not take place until after the death of Hongxi, who was replaced by the Xuande Emperor. In

1431, the fleet left and sailed for the Indian Ocean, making stops at the kingdoms of insular Southeast Asia along the way. The result of the seven voyages was that China had established itself with other major powers as a formidable force that needed to be recognized. Although the fleet was largely a treasure fleet with diplomatic intentions, it was also largely a military fleet that sought to intimidate the foreigners.

In fact, the military contingent that made up the fleet would also help combat the pirates and illicit trade that had begun developing in the southern waters by Guangdong. The Japanese had also taken to piracy along these southern coasts, and although Admiral Zheng He did not actively attempt to eliminate the threat of pirates in these regions, this huge naval force did manage to inspire terror to anyone who laid eyes on it, whether pirate or a foreign port. There were several instances of pirates attempting to capture treasure ships; however, Zheng He laid waste to these pirates and essentially secured the maritime routes for trade.

China had become economically and technologically advanced compared to civilizations in Europe at the time, and the fleet, which had reached a total of 3,500 ships, was unmatched by any other world power. Nevertheless, the fleet never made an eighth voyage, and the ships were either burned in the docks or left to rot. Xuande believed that the tributes that were being sent to him and China were unnecessary and were being carried out on behalf of his grandfather's wishes rather than his own. In the end, Xuande sided with his father's belief that the voyages should cease. Xuande felt that the policies established by the Hongwu Emperor were more in line with the way the empire should be run, and so China began to revert to the xenophobic policies of Hongwu and reduce its presence in other lands. By 1525, the largest naval fleet in the world had essentially been destroyed or dismantled by China itself. On top of that, the records and maps of Zheng He were confiscated by the Ministry of War in 1477.

The Arrival of Europeans

While China was in the process of isolating itself from the rest of the world, the European explorers were beginning to discover new lands, such as North America and South America. Among the countries doing the most exploring during this time were the Portuguese. The Portuguese had reached India in 1498, and by 1509 they had established part of their empire in India. This allowed the Portuguese to have a base of operations to further expand east into Asia. In 1511, the Portuguese captured the large spice trading center of Malacca in Malaysia, and like their base in India, Malacca allowed the Portuguese to have a foothold, thereby providing access to China and Southeast Asia (Brinkley 1904).

The Portuguese explorer Jorge Álvares visited the Chinese coast in 1513 and was the first European to do so via the sea. Shortly after, more Portuguese visited around the Tunmen Inlet, which is believed to have been somewhere around the Pearl River Delta, and an establishment was set up there in 1514. At this time the Chinese knew nothing of the Portuguese other than their violent takeover of Malacca, a tributary to the Chinese Empire, so the Portuguese were treated with caution.

In 1516, Rafael Perestrello was dispatched from Malacca to the islands of Guangdong where his people were well received. Due to this favorable reception, more ships and trading vessels were sent the following year under the command of Perez de Andrade. The fleet anchored on the island Shang-chuan and was at first viewed with suspicion, given the frequent raids from Japanese pirates around the Guangdong region. However, Andrade was peaceful in his dealings with the Chinese and the Chinese allowed two of his ships to proceed to Guangzhou, while the others returned to Malacca or sailed up the coast with Chinese junks to other merchant factories. The peaceful interactions with the Portuguese was not to last for very long thanks to Andrade's brother, Simão de Andrade, also known as Simon (Brinkley 1904: 170-142).

The Portuguese fleet that arrived in 1518 under the command of Andrade's brother quickly turned to piracy, and the diplomatic relations between the Chinese and Portuguese deteriorated. At the time, an envoy was in Beijing, where they had been peacefully welcomed, but after hearing news of the actions of Portuguese (led by Simão de Andrade), the Chinese demanded of the visiting envoy that the Portuguese leave Malacca (since it was a tributary of China). The envoy refused and was thrown in prison, where one of the Portuguese diplomats was executed. The rest of the envoy was eventually shipped off to prison in Guangzhou.

The hostile activities of the Portuguese are mainly attributed to Simão de Andrade, who was accused of kidnapping Chinese boys and girls for prostitution, although he is also said to have attempted establishing a fort on one of the islands. The establishment of a fort would have been viewed as a hostile invasion on the part of the Portuguese, much the same way Malacca was invaded. The Chinese retaliated in 1521 by sending a fleet of junks to the Portuguese settlement and attacking them. The Portuguese were killed in the region or retreated to non-Chinese ports. The Chinese then issued a policy prohibiting anyone with European characteristics from entering Guangzhou or Guangdong.

The Portuguese would have completely lost their foothold in China were it not for the corruption and bribery that saturated the administrative system in Guangzhou (Smith 1920: 9). Despite the laws and regulations regarding dealings with foreigners, by 1537 three settlements had been established in the nearby region: Shang-chuan, Lang-peh-kao (Lampaçao), and Macao, which was established entirely on lies told to the Chinese. The Portuguese had told officials that tribute to the Chinese (which was in fact normal trading goods) had become wrecked in storms and needed to be dried. The Portuguese were allowed to erect sheds and structures for this purpose at Macao, but numerous merchants established themselves as tenants there and managed to pay the Chinese a yearly rent of 500 ounces of silver. The location of Macao was beneficial and strategically chosen by the Portuguese, as it was in close communication with Guangzhou and connected via a river system. In contrast to their earlier dealings with the Chinese, the

Portuguese attempted to appear more humble and comply with the wishes of the Chinese rather than with force.

The suspicions that the Chinese had of the foreigners never went away and were only fueled as other European empires came into contact with China. The Spanish, for example, had been paying for Chinese exports with silver from the New World (mainly Mexico) through their base in Manila. The Chinese believed that this silver must have come from Manila and the Chinese population in the Philippines began looking for the source of the valuable metals. Suspicion from the Spaniards reached a breaking point in 1603 when they massacred all of the Chinese on the islands. Furthermore, whenever a Chinese merchant vessel came to trade in the islands, the number of Chinese people was limited, and they were heavily taxed.

Between 1635 and 1637, a fleet of four ships from the British Empire reached Macao under the command of Captain John Weddell. The captain's dealings with the Portuguese were hindered since they saw the English as commercial rivals, so Weddell brought his fleet to nearby Guangzhou. Although Weddell had made his peaceful intentions clear, the Portuguese had secretly been feeding the Chinese authorities misinformation as to the intents of the new foreigners. The result was a brief exchange of cannon fire and raiding between the two sides. After the exchange of gunfire and raiding, the Chinese agreed that the cargoes of the ships could be sold. The merchants who had accompanied Weddell felt that future hostilities should be avoided and that it would be far easier to pay off the officials of Guangzhou; in their minds, any money lost from the bribes would quickly be made back through trade (Smith 1920: 11).

Needless to say, not all of the English merchants were fully convinced that trade with the Chinese was worth the effort, and another trading fleet from the British would not reach China until 1664. Unfortunately for the British, the Portuguese again convinced the Chinese that the British were thieves and violent people, resulting in poor trading opportunities for the East India Company (Brinkley 1904: 188-189).

Concerning the actions by the Portuguese, Sir John Davis, second Governor of Hong Kong, wrote, "In the progress of all these trials one of the most striking circumstances is the stupid pertinacity with which the Portuguese at Macao excluded English ships from that port, and the perfidy with which they represented their supposed rivals to the Chinese with a view to prevent their getting a footing at Canton.... Their systematic policy has been to attribute motives to the English which should injure them with the provincial Government." (Brinkley 1904: 192).

Near the end of the 17th century, the English were on uneasy terms with the Chinese but still trading regularly in Guangzhou. During this time, there was no establishment of rules or regulations regarding trade between Chinese merchants and the East India Company, which had been given a monopoly over trading in the region by the British Government. Moreover, there were no clear rules regarding daily life between the foreigners and the Chinese. At times, the British would obey certain Chinese laws, while other Chinese laws were ignored in favor of

British laws. The East India Company tried to add stability to the region by empowering representatives with consular authority, but the Chinese never acknowledged this power. In the eyes of the Chinese, the foreigners were regarded as "barbarians" and were in need of a higher civilization, such as the Chinese. As a result, life in Guangzhou was relatively lawless, with merchants and sailors doing as they pleased. The threat of the Chinese ceasing trade with the merchants due to the British breaking Chinese laws was always a possibility, but the reality of the situation was that the Chinese merchants and administration was becoming increasingly wealthy through trades, tariffs and bribes.

The English merchants gradually began to settle in Guangzhou, or Canton as it was known to the English; taking on wives from the local Chinese population and setting up establishments to teach English. Trade began growing between the two Empires, and the first English man-of-war ship would arrive in the waters of China in 1742.

During the 17th century, as foreigners began encroaching on Chinese lands and attempted to open up favorable trade, the Ming dynasty was in decline and shifting to the Qing dynasty. The Qing dynasty had already been founded in 1636 by the Jurchen Aisin Gioro, a Manchuria clan who were not Han Chinese. The Manchu state was founded by Nurhaci in the region of Jianzhou. Nurhaci declared himself Khan of the Great Jin after consolidating power in the region. The Manchus were few, ethnically speaking, but they added Mongols and Han Chinese to their fighting regiments, including an artillery corps made entirely out of Han Chinese.

In 1618, Nurhaci declared seven grievances against the Ming dynasty and began to seize Ming cities. In 1626, he was injured in the Battle of Ningyuan and died shortly afterwards, but despite this setback, the cities that the Manchu had captured were never recaptured by the Ming. Over the next few decades, Manchu forces sporadically raided and captured cities and land from the Ming dynasty. By 1644, the Ming dynasty was suffering heavily from ecological problems such as drought and famine, while the people in the north began rebelling against the administration. One rebel leader, Li Zicheng, breached the walls of Beijing. Rather than be captured by the rebels, the last emperor of the Ming dynasty hanged himself near the Forbidden City.

Upon hearing that the capital had fallen, Ming general Wu Sangui took his regiment from north of the Great Wall to try and stop the rebels. The rebels responded by sending troops from Beijing to attack Wu. In doing so, Wu had left the region north of the Great Wall unprotected, effectively handing the region over to the Qing. Although Wu had largely been successful in battling the rebels with his well-trained troops, he requested help from the Qing. In response, the Qing Empire decided that it would claim the throne (or Mandate of Heaven as it was known) for itself, and it asked Wu to fight for the Qing. Wu surrendered his army to the Qing, and together they beat back the rebel forces to Beijing. The rebels looted what they could from Beijing and fled while the Qing army claimed the capital and the surrounding regions.

Those who were still loyal in the Ming army established a new base in Nanjing. This base was short-lived and captured in 1645, and the Prince of Fu, Zhu Yousong, who had been enthroned, was captured. After the fall of Nanjing, a new court emerged with another self-proclaimed heir to the throne. This new court was held in Fuzhou with Zhu Yujian, Prince of Tang, proclaiming himself the new Longwu Emperor of the Ming. The court was swiftly captured by the Qing in 1646, during which Zhu Yujian's younger brother, Zhu Yuyue, fled to Guangzhou. Zhu Yuyue established the Yongli court there, but he fled in 1647 when the Qing occupied the region.

The Longwu Emperor

The commander of the occupying Qing forces was Li Chengdong, who went about suppressing the Ming loyalists in the Guangdong region. After conquering the region, he himself rebelled against the Qing and established his own rule in the region. This simultaneous rebellion left only scattered Qing forces in the Guangdong region, but by 1649 the Qing armies of the North had managed to retake Guangdong and its surrounding regions. Upon the capture of Guangzhou, after a nearly year-long siege, a majority of the population was massacred. Nevertheless, Ming loyalists occasionally attempted to retake the cities, but these attacks were unsuccessful. It was not until 1683 that the last remaining claimants to the Ming dynasty were captured or died, and the Qing were able to conquer China.

With such continuous turmoil going on in China during the transition from the Ming to the Qing dynasty, it is no wonder that foreigners were able to take advantage of local officials to bribe their way into the ports. However, by the end of the 17th century, the Qing dynasty was firmly established and could focus on establishing set guidelines to deal with foreign merchants in Guangzhou.

In 1661, Xuanye became the Kangxi Emperor (reigning from 1661-1722). He faced the challenge of merging his Manchu regime with the Han Chinese. The people of the southern regions, especially Guangdong, still longed for the Han rulers of the Qing dynasty and so strict measures were taken to prevent rebellions there. The Kangxi emperor feared that if left unchecked, a naval fleet could develop there that would be difficult to suppress. After the final rebellions were stopped in 1683 and China was once again unified, a series of custom stations were opened in Guangzhou and Macao, as well as other port cities. In 1685, foreign traders were allowed to officially enter these restricted ports.

The Kangxi Emperor

A trading company was specifically set up in Guangzhou in 1686, known as the Yánghuò Háng, or Ocean Trading House, to deal with foreign traders. Chinese merchants would need to visit the Yánghuò Háng to pay taxes due on imports and exports. This basic system essentially allowed Kangxi to keep the foreign trade market under control. Conflict only began to emerge when Pope Clement XI condemned Chinese worship, resulting in Kangxi expelling almost all missionaries from his court and leading to more xenophobia in the Qing court.

The Yánghuò Háng continued largely unchanged in Guangzhou until 1745, when the Qianlong Emperor (who reigned from 1735-1796) made individual Chinese merchants responsible for the foreign merchants and vessels they dealt with in Guangzhou. These Chinese merchants would be in charge of paying the taxes they owed, as well as of collecting import and export taxes from the foreign traders. In 1760, with permission from the government, a group of Chinese merchants came together to act as mediators between all foreign trade and the court. This group of merchants formed a monopoly on trade and would do the purchasing of goods for the foreigners, while dealing with the taxes and duties involved with the trades. Since this group of merchants, known as the Cohong, would be sanctioned by the Qing court, they had the authority to impose taxes however they wanted. This meant that the Western merchants would not be able to negotiate prices or try to cut deals with the Chinese merchants, as the prices were fixed.

The Qing court now had even greater control over how foreigners could trade, much to the frustration of Western merchants. Moreover, foreign merchants were restricted in their ability to travel within China and largely had to lodge their complaints with the authorities in Guangzhou. It was Chinese protocol that Westerners should have no direct dealings or contact with Beijing, unless for tribute or through official diplomats. When merchants, such as the English merchant James Flint, attempted to make contact with the Qianlong emperor, thereby breaking protocol, the emperor declared all ports in the north closed to foreign ships. Thus, in 1757, all merchant ships were to conduct their business through the Guangzhou port. This new system would be known to Westerners as the Canton System.

Flint, the English merchant who had continuously left Canton despite warnings, unsuccessfully attempted to open the ports of Zhejiang, which resulted in further restrictions being placed on trade. These new rules were known as the "Five Counter-Measures Against the Barbarians." These measures mandated the following: foreigners could not trade in Guangzhou during the winter; foreign merchants needed to stay in set locations to be monitored by the Cohong; Chinese locals could not borrow money; Chinese locals could not work for foreigners or inform themselves of the trade markets from the foreigners; and foreign merchant vessels had to dock in a specific location to await inspection by officials.

The East India Company continued to protest these restrictions and taxations. The complaints largely fell on deaf ears, but the British market was in demand for Chinese tea, leaving the East India Company little choice but to comply with the restrictions and taxes. Much to the outrage of the British, they felt that these restrictions did not put them on equal terms with the Chinese. This assumption was correct, for the Chinese court viewed Qing culture as superior to Western cultures. The British, on the other hand, viewed their culture as superior to the Chinese and felt that the trade market should be open and free rather than restricted and controlled by the Qing court. Furthermore, the superior attitude the Chinese court had regarding its culture was reflected in the lack of demands for British products. In fact, the Cohong demanded that silver should be used for trade rather than other English products. These restrictions imposed by the Qing court, as well as British demand for tea, would provide some of the underlying causes of the Opium Wars between the two sides.

War

Despite all the tensions, trade carried on, and by the 19th century, Chinese tea, silks and porcelain were still in high demand in Britain, while there remained no demand from the Chinese for British products. For much of the 18th century, the East India Company was forced to ship boatloads of silver to China rather than manufactured goods, resulting in a deficit in trade and a strain on the economy. The East India Company, which had its own naval and military force, was also in debt from wars being fought to control trade in India. To stop this debt from increasing, the East India Company, which still had a monopoly on trade in the region, began smuggling opium into Guangzhou (opium had been illegal in China since 1729). By 1793, the East India Company had created a monopoly on the purchase of opium in Bengal, India, thereby cutting out the Bengali merchants from the trade. The opium produced in Bengal was then sold in Calcutta (since it could not be sold in China) under the condition that it be sent to China. The East India Company would not carry the drug on their own ships and instead used private vessels so that they could deny any wrongdoing if the situation called for it. Smugglers then brought the opium to Lintin Island near Guangzhou, where it was sold. Profits from the opium was then used to purchase Chinese goods. It is estimated that around 900 tons of opium were being smuggled into China annually. Although the drug was already illegal in China, the Jiaqing Emperor (who reigned from 1796 to 1820) declared in 1799 that the import of opium was illegal. This did little to deter the buying and selling of the drug. In the early 19th century, large amounts of silver were being shipped from Guangzhou to India, resulting in a drain on the Chinese economy.

In exchange for the illegal drug, the British demanded silver, which in turn was used to purchase tea and other Chinese goods. By 1838, the East India Company no longer had to send any silver laden ships - it could rely entirely on the selling of opium to purchase tea.

The use of opium in Guangzhou did not originate with the British; in fact, it was the Portuguese who had first begun bringing the drug into the country. The import of the drug was initially for medicinal purposes. As a medicine, the drug was imported by the Portuguese beginning with around 200 chests (each chest weighing 133 pounds) in 1730, increasing to 1,000 chests brought in during 1767 (Brinkley 1904: 236). However, by the end of the century the British had finished their conquest of Bengal in India and dominated the opium import business in Guangzhou. The difference in the import methods of the British from the Portuguese began to cause unwanted attention. Whereas the Portuguese had gradually increased the number of chests being brought in so as to make the drug still appear as a medicine, the British began importing large quantities that could not possibly be used for medicine. Once this occurred, the British were forced to bribe officials, but the bribes were trivial given the overall profits that the drug was able to pull in.

The British government and the East India Company were well aware of the illicit practices. One British merchant in Guangzhou wrote to Parliament in 1782, "The importation of opium to China is forbidden on very severe penalties: the opium on seizure is burned; the vessel in which it is brought to the port confiscated, and the Chinese in whose possession it is found for sale is punishable with death. It might be concluded that with a law so rigid no foreigners would venture to import, nor any Chinese dare to purchase, this article. Yet opium for a long course of time has been annually carried to China, and often in large quantities, both by our country's vessels and those of the Portuguese. It is sometimes landed at Macao and sometimes at Whampoa equally liable to the above penalties in either port, as the Portuguese are, so to say, entirely under the Chinese rule. That this contraband trade has hitherto been carried on without incurring the penalties of the law is owing to the excess of corruption in the executive part of the Chinese Government. ... In the year 1780 a new Viceroy was appointed to the Government of Canton; this man had the reputation of an upright, bold, and rigid Minister. I was informed that he had information of these illicit, practices and was resolved to take cognizance of them." (Brinkley 1904: 238).

In the early 19th century, smugglers had taken control of Lintin Island, which lay between Macao and the river of Guangzhou. Heavily armed boats guarded the island in open defiance of government officials. The government of Guangzhou at times either did not have the resources to counter these smugglers and their vessels, or was in fact in on the entire operation and chose not to use its resources even when they were available. From here, the illegal drug could be "taxed" by the officials, a tax which would take the form of silver or the drug itself. The drug could then be loaded onto Chinese vessels and brought into Guangzhou. Control and order was what the East India Company desired and even in the realm of bribery and corruption, the East India Company managed to create a relatively smooth system. There were instances of Chinese locals being shot and killed by people on the smuggling boats. This tended to cause a series of escalating retaliations between the smugglers and the coastal villages.

In 1834, the East India Company's charter expired and they no longer had a monopoly over trade in Guangzhou. As a result, private merchants hauling opium flooded the market. With the end of the East India Company's established order, private merchants decided to bypass Lintin Island and instead began shipping the drug directly into Guangzhou with their own foreign armed vessels. These brazen acts could not be overlooked, and the government in Beijing quickly became aware of the situation.

Meanwhile, there was no British superintendent to oversee trade as there had been when the East India Company had been in charge. The British, however, were silent on the subject. The British government was content to let British subjects live on foreign shores and carry on illicit trade with no British authority to redress the situation, or for the Chinese officials to appeal to. This undiplomatic approach was taken as an insult by the Chinese, who had to take more extreme measures to deal with the opium problem in Guangzhou.

It was not until 1837 that Captain Charles Elliot became the British superintendent and reestablished communications with the Chinese and took up residence in Guangzhou. Captain Elliot was interested in trying to recreate the relationship with the Chinese merchants and administration that had been in place during the monopoly of the East India Company. Captain Elliot had no sympathy for the smugglers of Lintin Island or for the opium drug, but he had relatively little power to do anything against the approximately 50 armed British, American and Portuguese vessels that surrounded the island. Furthermore, Elliot was not satisfied to deal with the Cohong merchants who were conveying communications from the Chinese government. Elliot felt that he should only receive communications directly from the Chinese government, thereby putting them on equal terms. Reluctantly, the Chinese government agreed and the Cohong were bypassed.

Elliot

During the 1830s, the British government sent numerous appointed officials to speak with the Chinese government directly regarding trading agreements. This however, was not to the liking of the Chinese government, which had been used to dealing with only British merchant managers and even then through the Cohong and not directly. These British officials were meant to show that the British government was trying to stop or prevent the trade of opium, but in reality, these officials had very little power to carry out any enforcement (Lovell 2015).

The Chinese government had begun to enforce its rules and regulations with greater fervor. In 1839, Elliot reported that opium trade in the region had stalled as the users of the drug were being locked up and more and more shipments were being turned back or destroyed (Cameron 1991). This was seen as a setback to the British government, which, without the income from opium, would need to find another source of money to buy tea. The importation of tea was of course a source of income itself for the British government, which taxed the imported good.

In response to the flood of opium being brought into the country, the death penalty was imposed by the Daoguang Emperor (who reigned from 1820-1850) on any dealers of the drug. Opium dealers would be strangled in public while native vessels that carried the drug would be seized and burned. The drastic methods that the Chinese were taking to crack down on opium dealing had little effect on foreign merchants or the British government. The British Secretary of State for Foreign Affairs, Lord Palmerston, related to Parliament that despite these increased measures, the Chinese were not really sincere in their efforts to eradicate the opium trade and would in fact be upset if the opium market were to disappear. As for the users of the drug itself, there was no punishment outlined initially as it was thought that the user had punished themselves enough by taking the drug (Brinkley 1904: 235). The initial laws that were established in the 18th century had dealt primarily in dealing with the sellers of the drug who were local Chinese pushers or opium den owners. The idea of dealing with the foreign merchants who provided the drug to the Chinese was not a topic that was addressed until the 19th century.

In an attempt to awe the foreigners with the seriousness of their determination, the administration of Guangzhou proclaimed that the first native to be caught dealing the drug would be publicly executed in view of the foreign factories. When the execution was to take place, the foreigners were appalled and went about chasing away the executioner and his followers, as well as the Chinese locals who had gathered to watch the execution. The locals, however, fought back and forced the foreigners back into their factories until Chinese soldiers arrived to break up the mob. Captain Elliot was under strict orders to allow no protection to British subjects if they were caught breaking Chinese laws, and ordered the opium carrying vessels to leave the ports of Guangzhou. The smugglers, however, knew that Captain Elliot had no real power to enforce this and continued to do as they pleased. Even if Captain Elliot had been successful or forced the smugglers from Guangzhou, they simply would have gone back to conducting business on Lintin Island.

To continue to battle the opium trade, a special commissioner was appointed to deal with problem in Guangzhou. Lin Zexu was appointed as Commissioner in 1839 and when he arrived in Guangzhou the smuggling ships had already gradually retreated to Lintin Island. When Captain Elliot was urged to deal with the illegal trade, he replied that he only had authority over legitimate trade. In return Lin demanded that all of the opium on Lintin Island be delivered to him, and that all of the foreign merchants should sign bonds stating that they would not import opium. In order to pressure Captain Elliot and the merchants, he severed communication with the foreigners in the factories and the ships, thereby essentially "trapping" the foreigners in Guangzhou. If the demands were not met in three days, Lin threatened to execute two of the major Cohong merchants (Elleman 2001: 16). 1,037 chests of opium were given over in order to delay these executions, and it is likely that Lin saw the futility of executing Chinese merchants to punish the foreigners.

While the anti-opium campaign was taking place in China, there were a number of environmental factors that were weakening the government. There had been a series of extreme droughts that had ruined crops, resulting in famine. The result of this among the Chinese people was civil unrest and a weakening of the empire's military forces. In the Guangzhou region, the anti-opium measures were scoffed at by the Western communities as merchants in Britain pushed for freedom of trade and the legalization of the opium trade. In China, a large council of officials from all over held a debate regarding the opium crisis. The result was the positioning of Lin Zexu, former Governor of Hubei and Hunan, as Imperial Commissioner. He was tasked with the suppression of opium trade (Mao 2005).

Lin Zexu

Lin Zexu arrived in Guangzhou in early 1839 and began implementing his strict plan for dealing with the opium crisis. His plan would deal not only with the local dealers and users of the drug, but also with the foreign merchants themselves. His dealings with foreign merchants were misguided, as he was only informed of the foreigners through second-hand knowledge and had no direct dealings himself. Therefore, he assumed, based on his lack of knowledge, that the diet of the British merchants was reliant on tea and rhubarb, and that if these key dietary elements were removed, the British would be forced to leave or submit. Lin Zexu was also confused in the ways of British trading by assuming that the merchants were following orders of the government – put simply, he failed to fully understand that the selling of opium provided the merchants with profits that were then used to buy tea (Lovell 2015). Nevertheless, he did uphold the notion that foreigners must follow Chinese laws on Chinese land.

In March, Lin Zexu ordered that the Westerns should deliver the supplies of opium that they had with them, and until that was carried out, all trade would cease with the Westerners. This blockade of trade lasted for 47 days until Elliot forfeited 20,283 cases of British opium. This may have been seen by the Chinese as a significant win in their prevention of smuggling, but as was noted earlier, the opium trade had already stalled for the British and what was handed over to Lin Zexu had been sitting in the harbor unable to be sold for the last five months.

Lin Zexu had succeeded in ridding the region of opium, but he was still tasked with preventing even more opium from entering the country. Meanwhile, the entire situation did not sit well with Elliot or the British in general, who viewed themselves as superior to the Chinese and thus did not like being treated as "barbarians." Back in Britain, politics were being influenced by pamphlets printed by parties with vested interest in the conditions to which the merchants were being treated during the blockade. It was being spread around Britain that merchants were being "imprisoned" in "appalling conditions," including the deprivation of food and water. For good measure, the pamphlets even asserted that the merchants were regularly being threatened with death. The reality was that the merchants were being well taken care of with food and water, and they even had Chinese servants.

As this was going on, other merchants in England applied further pressure to the government, claiming that the cotton trade in India was being destroyed because the opium growers and suppliers there could no longer afford to buy cotton from the British (from the profits that they would have gained from selling opium). It was put to the Foreign Secretary in September of 1839 that China should issue an apology for the perceived insult to the British, repay the merchants for the loss of opium, and negotiate a favorable trade treaty that would open more ports.

When Captain Elliot arrived in Guangzhou from Macao, Commissioner Lin perceived the move as the beginning of the withdrawal of the British from Guangzhou. Captain Elliot had secretly instructed British vessels, smugglers included, to retreat to the island of Hong Kong and prepare to resist the Chinese. He had also secretly sent a dispatch requesting a British Man-of-War vessel for protection. Commissioner Lin had the foreign factories surrounded with armed forces and made the foreigners sign his bond swearing to never trade in opium. He then went further and demanded all the opium be delivered to the Guangzhou port, a demand that Captain Elliot reluctantly met. Captain Elliot had promised the merchants credit, on behalf of the Crown, for their opium and 20,283 chests of opium were surrendered (British Parliamentary Papers, 1840). Captain Elliot had hoped that by surrendering the opium, the foreigners within the factories would be allowed to leave at will and that trade could resume as normal.

The opium was stored on 22 vessels, 40 miles down the river of Guangzhou, and Commissioner Lin would not end his siege until he had received the contraband. This delay lasted roughly 48 days. Considering the numerous promises that the British had broken with the

Chinese and the fact that Captain Elliot had plans to resist the Chinese with force, Lin was justified in not releasing any foreigners until his demands were met. Once the demands were met, trade resumed in Guangzhou under the close watch of Lin. What Lin found upon inspecting the records of the Cohong merchants and their dealings with the foreigners was that for the 20 years it had been illegal for foreign vessels to carry opium up the river, the Cohong merchants had never turned one away (Fay 1975: 144). This obvious infraction against the law prompted Lin to create a new bond for the merchants: punishment for dealing opium was death.

The British strongly opposed such extreme measures which they felt went against the principle of free trade, although non-opium dealing merchants had no problems with signing such a bond. Lin's crackdown on the drug caused the black market to flourish as demand for the drug was great, yet supply was more scarce than it had been before. Smuggling activities continued on Lintin Island much as they had in the past, and the Cohong were still willing to risk death for the profits that the drug would bring in.

The British continued to trade with the Chinese and to obey local laws only when they saw fit. In the summer of 1839, in the nearby port town of Kowloon, two British sailors from the ship *Carnatic* became intoxicated on *samshu* (a strong rice liquor) and murdered one of the Chinese locals (Fey 1975: 171). Elliot had the sailors arrested and paid compensation to the family, but he refused to hand over the guilty Englishmen to the Chinese. The penalty for the Englishmen would have been death, and for Elliot to not hand over the guilty parties was viewed by Lin as disobeying Chinese law. In retaliation, Lin gave orders to Chinese workers from Macao, and entry to the Pearl River was blockaded by Chinese war junks. The British in turn recalled their ships from the Chinese coast while the Chinese denied British ships from docking in Macao.

The British were now effectively stranded at sea with little in the way of provisions and a finite supply of freshwater. The 50-cannon frigate *HMS Volage* arrived shortly after to help protect the some 50-60 British ships from potential Chinese attack (Elleman 2001: 17). The Chinese did allow the British to obtain the most basic of supplies, but were denied any access to the port towns. Frustrated with the inability to purchase supplies, Elliot threatened that if supplies could not be purchased by 3:00 pm, the British would open fire on Kowloon. After his demands were not met, the British and Chinese exchanged cannon and gun fire. At the end of the day, in what would be known as the Battle of Kowloon, the Chinese junks had retreated, and the British could purchase supplies from the town. Despite this defeat, the Chinese commanders reported an overwhelming victory, claiming to have sunk a large British warship and killing up to 50 sailors (Elleman 2001: 18). They also claimed that the British were unable to gain the supplies that they had sought.

In reality, the British came out of the battle virtually unharmed. The idea of a Chinese victory may have stemmed from the point in the battle when the British had begun to run low on ammunition. Two of the three vessels, the *Louisa* and the *Pearl* (the third being the *Volage*), had begun a retreat when they had run low on ammunition. The Chinese, who had a sense of pride in "repelling barbarians," saw this as a victory. Upon pursuit of the retreating British ships, the Chinese junks were fired upon by the *Louisa* and *Pearl*, which were also joined by two smaller British vessels. The victory reported to Commissioner Lin was passed on to Beijing, which gave the emperor a false view of the vastly superior British forces. The habit of reporting defeats as victories likely assisted in many of the battles in the Opium Wars being one-sided, as the Chinese commanders did not learn from past military engagements with the British.

Tensions between the Chinese and British were high, but some non-opium dealing merchants felt that they had a right to sign the bond of Commissioner Lin and sell their goods in Guangzhou. One merchant vessel owned by British Quakers had signed the bond, prompting Elliot to issue his own blockade to Guangzhou. As a result, there were accusations from the Chinese that Elliot's blockade prevented trade, while the British claimed that Lin's blockade was preventing trade. When another British vessel attempted to follow the precedent established by the Quaker merchants, Elliot ordered the merchant vessel to be fired upon. Mistaking the warning shots across the bow of the ship for acts of war, Chinese junks moved in to protect the merchant vessel. The Chinese junks bore red flags which were interpreted in the European sense as declaring war (whereas the white indicated peace), thus beginning the First Battle of Chuanbi on November 3, 1839.

The battle itself was technically between the British ships and the rogue British merchant ship, but the 16 Chinese junks and 13 fireships that came to the aid of the British merchants were outmatched by the two man-of-war ships *Volage* and *Hyacinth*. The British warships were more maneuverable than the Chinese ships and were able to destroy a fireboat and a war junk during the first barrage against the slow Chinese vessels. In the second barrage, the Chinese fleet was in confusion, and another Chinese warship was blown up and three were sunk while several others were damaged. The *Volage* received light damage and the mizzenmast of the *Hyacinth* had been struck (Elleman 2001: 20). Nevertheless, the Chinese military reported greater damage to the British fleet, making the battle seem as though it was another military victory for the Chinese.

Out of fear for future retaliation against British ships, Elliot moved his fleet away from Chuanbi and attempted to make port in Macao. The Portuguese were unwilling to risk conflict with the Chinese and denied them entry, while the Daoguang Emperor proclaimed that no foreigner should offer assistance to the British. In Guangzhou, the Chinese navy, under the command of Admiral Guan Tianpei, believed that they had repelled the British, so few preparations were made for defense. Meanwhile the British were not interested in a full-scale war and treated the conflicts as punitive expeditions. Ships and troops from around the British Empire were gathered, although naval forces were more concerned with conflicts elsewhere at the time. By June 1840, the British had assembled enough forces to begin their offensive against the Chinese. An ultimatum was issued, demanding that the Qing pay compensation for the loss of opium and halt in trade. Additionally, a letter from Lord Palmerston reached the Emperor blaming all of the events on Commissioner Lin. The authorities of Guangzhou readily rejected the demands, and the emperor wrote to Lin, "Externally you wanted to stop the [opium] trade, but it has not been stopped; internally you wanted to wipe out the outlaws [opium smugglers and smokers], but they are not cleared away. You are just making excuses with empty words. Nothing has been accomplished but many troubles have been created. Thinking of these things, I cannot contain my rage. What do you have to say now?" (Elleman 2001: 21).

In Guangzhou, Lin issued a reward for captured or killed British soldiers, while the emperor called for reinforcements on land and sea. The British had already captured the city of Dinghai on the large island of Zhoushan, while Chinese forces had surrounded Macao, creating what was termed the "barrier." On August 19, 1840, British forces attacked the 9 war junks and 1,500 Chinese troops that made up the "barrier." Around 200 marines were aboard the *Enterprise* steamer, followed by two long boats in tow and several corvettes. When close to the barrier, which had been designed to protect the city walls and not the sea, the corvettes opened fire, forcing the Chinese gun crew to flee. The British marines then landed and set up artillery, while two of the slow moving war junks were sunk and the rest retreated. The British had won the Battle of the Barrier with light casualties and proceeded to destroy the supplies and magazines of the Chinese. The emperor was told of a great Chinese victory, which supposedly incurred many British casualties and their retreat, yet the Chinese never attempted to take control of Macao again.

In October 1840, Lin was relieved of his duties as Commissioner and governor-general of the Guangdong region and summoned to Beijing for trial. Qishan assumed the vacated position left by Lin. By the beginning of 1841, two forts guarding the port of Guangzhou had been taken by the British, forcing Qishan to sign, on January 20, 1841, the Convention of Chuanbi. This convention, drawn by the British, ceded Hong Kong to the British, forced the Qing to pay $6 million for the conflict, and allowed the British to communicate directly with Chinese officials in Guangzhou.

This rather humiliating convention was swiftly denounced by the emperor, and Qishan was dismissed from his post and deported (Fay 1975). The successor of Qishan mounted an attack on Elliot at Guangzhou, compelling the British to move to Hong Kong. Elliot had wished to spare the city from becoming occupied by troops, but Palmerston had been displeased with the way in which Elliot had handled the situation, believing that Elliot had been too soft on the Chinese and that more force should have been used, particularly with the Convention of Chuanbi (Cameron 1991). As a result, Elliot was dismissed from his position. It is likely that Palmerston, who thought he could control the situation from Britain, believed he could scare the Chinese into submission with the more advanced fleet and became upset with the situation when this did not occur.

To the rest of the world, this conflict with China revealed crucial weaknesses within the Chinese empire. The Chinese navy was considerably inferior to the vessels that Western countries were producing, the fleet itself had no central base and could be stationed far away from safe havens, and the coast of China was too much for such a small number of ships to protect. To the powers in the West, these battles made the Chinese seem weak and their lands free for the taking. Despite the lack of agreement in London over the validity of the Convention, Commodore J. J. Bremer sent Captain Edward Belcher out with a dispatch of soldiers to claim Hong Kong Island for the British, and on January 26, 1841, the island was formally considered by some as part of the British Empire.

Belcher

Following the collapse of the convention, foreign factories were taken over in Guangzhou by the British. A large portion of the Chinese junks were sunk, and the shore batteries of Guangzhou were destroyed. Guangzhou was surrounded with British troops, and the newly created shallow-draft steamer, the *Nemesis*, moved up river northwest to deploy more troops. Guangzhou could now easily be taken over by the British.

On May 21, 1841, the Chinese military fortified within Guangzhou, which was partially occupied by the British, and launched a surprise attack on the British. The British factories of Guangzhou were overtaken by the Qing, and hidden artillery attacked the navy from the Pearl River and from within the city (MacPherson 1842: 120-135). Major General Hugh Gough of the British navy had pulled his forces back to the island of Hong Kong to regroup and launch a counterattack on Guangzhou. After roughly a week of fighting with very few casualties or damages caused to the British, the city was virtually under their control. As one witness wrote of the capture, "The city of Canton - that proud city, which had so often defied us and insulted our flag, whose population alone was nearly one million, and whose boasted army numbered 50,000, was now humbled before barely a 20th part of its strength. The flag of truce, that badge of peace, respected all over the world, but by the Chinese so frequently treated with contempt, was now seen to wave from the most conspicuous parts of the ramparts; at the same time, a blue-buttoned mandarin, advancing to one of the embrasures nearest to our position, and waving a white flag, seemed to implore an interview." (MacPherson 1842: 138).

19th century depiction of Guangzhou factories

Wishing to avoid another attack, officials from Guangzhou agreed to the three terms of peace designed by the British. The first was that the Qing commissioners and all of the troops proceed 60 miles away from the city within six days. The second required that $60 million be paid within a week as ransom for the city. Finally, until these demands were met, the British forces would stay where they were (MacPherson 1842: 142; Elleman 2001: 24). The demands were met, and British forces withdrew on May 31.

As with military failures, the Qing administration reported this diplomatic failure to the emperor as an overwhelming success. According to Rait (1903: 203), the emperor had been informed that the amount paid was for private debts and that the "barbarians" had begged for the emperor to show them mercy and have the debt repaid and allow commerce in Guangzhou to continue. As for the British, Major General Hugh Gough saw the actions undertaken by Captain Elliot (who at this point had not received word that he was relieved of his post and did not consult the military or navy regarding this ransom) as no better than a form of buccaneering (Rait 1903: 203).

Gough

During this time, the Portuguese had remained neutral, but following the British occupation of Dinghai and their acquisition of control over the waterways of Guangzhou, the Portuguese allowed the British to use the port of Macao. The British were now able to focus their efforts up the Pearl River by using Hong Kong as their base station. On July 29, 1841, Captain Elliot was replaced as Superintendent by Henry Pottinger, who had just arrived in Hong Kong. With control over the waterways, the British were able to economically cripple the Qing Empire by

35

blockading the ports of southern China and seizing barges of the Pearl River carrying tribute and taxes.

Pottinger

In July of 1842 the British fleet sailed up river and captured Zhenjiang resulting, in 36 British soldiers being killed, the highest number of casualties yet encountered by the British. From here, they were able to cut off grain supply distribution for the empire and advance towards Nanking. The Qing officials of Nanking intercepted the British officials in August and negotiated the Treaty of Nanking, thus ending what would later be known as the First Opium War on August 29, 1842.

The Treaty of Nanking ended the role of the Cohong in Guangzhou and the factory system, and allowed four more ports to be opened for trade. The Qing were also forced to pay for the opium that Lin Zexu had destroyed earlier. The sums amounted to 6 million silver dollars, $3 million for the debts of British merchants, and $12 million for the cost of the war.

Rebellions

The opening of additional trade ports for foreigners meant that Guangzhou would no longer be the central focus of trade, but the region would soon be caught up in the Taiping Rebellion from 1850-1871. In order for the Qing Empire to pay war reparations, farmers were heavily taxed, and rents were raised. Further problems continued to accumulate with the continued importation of opium to the Guangdong region. In 1847, Hong Xiuquan, who believed himself to be the younger brother of Jesus and subsequently amassed a cult following, moved to Guangzhou to study the Bible. There he met with the American Baptist Issachar Jacox Roberts, who recognized the political motivations of Hong and refused to baptize him. Hong went on to create his own religion, mixing Christianity with Daoism and Confucianism, which would become known as the Taiping faith.

Hong Xiuquan

The Taiping Rebellion began with the routing of Qing forces by the Taiping in 1850 and the capture of Nanking in 1853. Under the religious-political ideology developed by Hong, the Manchu who ruled the Qing were seen as demons and as such had to be purged from China. By the end of the rebellion, roughly 20-30 million people had been killed based on this ideology (Platt 2012). Gradually, the forces were defeated, with Nanking being retaken in 1864 and the Taiping fleeing to the mountains of Guangdong.

Guangzhou would continue to be the center of the rebellions. In 1895, the Revive China Society began an uprising in the city. The society was based in Hong Kong and led by Lu Haodong, Yeung Ku-wan, and Sun Yat-sen, who planned to capture Guangzhou in a swift attack. The plans of their revolution were intercepted by the Qing administration, and the revolutionaries were captured. Lu Haodong was executed, while Sun Yat-sen went into exile. The Hong Kong government vowed that Yeung Ku-wan would never set foot in Qing territory again, but he was assassinated in 1901 by Qing agents in Hong Kong. This failed uprising would be known as the First Guangzhou Uprising, which would be followed by the second in 1911.

The Second Guangzhou Uprising was led by Huang Xing with the help of Sun Yat-sen. On April 27, 1911, Huang Xi stormed the residence of the Qing viceroy of the Guangdong region. The forces of the Qing eventually overwhelmed the roughly 100 revolutionaries, and many of them were killed. In total, 72 rebel bodies were identified, while the other bodies could not be found. In time, the 72 rebels would be recognized as martyrs, since it was believed that the Second Guangzhou Uprising was part of a series of uprisings that led the way for the Xinhai Revolution that successfully overthrew the Qing dynasty.

On December 29, 1911, Sun Yat-sen became the first provincial president of the newly established Republic of China; however, he would quickly cede power to Yuan Shikai. After some debate, Beijing became the capital of China, and the newly formed government began organizing itself internally. A new Chinese government would not formally be recognized by other world powers until 1928. During the period between 1912 and 1928, Guangzhou continued to be the center of rebellions.

Sun Yat-sen (sitting) with Chiang Kai-shek

A second revolution was organized after it was determined that Yuan had begun abusing his powers by ignoring parliament for making decisions. The Kuomintang of China was the nationalist party of China that formed shortly after Xinhai Revolution and formed the National Revolution Army. The party was founded by Song Jiaoren and Sun Yat-sen. Song was assassinated in 1913, prompting the ill-planned second revolution that failed. As a result, Sun fled to Japan and much of the Kuomintang of China party was expelled from China. Sun eventually established headquarters for the Kuomintang of China in Guangzhou in 1920.

In 1923, the government of Guangzhou and the Kuomintang of China began receiving assistance from the Soviet Union. Soviet advisers helped organize the Kuomintang of China and form cooperation with the Communist Party of China, thereby forming a united political front. In

1925, Sun died, and power of the party passed on to Chiang Kai-shek, who was in control of the military forces of Guangzhou. At this point, the surrounding warlords of the Guangdong province pledged their loyalty to the Kuomintang of China. Chiang then began to attack the northern government based in Beijing, and in 1928 he successfully took the capital.

During this chaotic period, the British in Guangzhou seemed relatively unfazed by the political turmoil going on around them. In 1920, C.A. Middleton Smith wrote about Guangzhou and its people, "At heart the Cantonese hates fighting, but somewhere in his complex nature there must be high courage or else a contempt for life, otherwise he could never remain under the present political conditions. If only he would also consider the welfare of his country, or even of his own province, he would be classed among the salt of the earth. Politically, Canton and its wealthy province is in chaos. In all other respects, Kwangtung (Guangdong) is fortunate. Richly endowed by nature, there is by water a natural method of transport for goods, a clever, industrious population, and a climate that is kind to crops. Its sea-coasts and the great port of Hong-Kong provide its people with unique opportunities for foreign intercourse. The best that we can hope is that the Cantonese will soon realize that nothing hinders progress so much as the intrigues of political factions, and nothing prevents men from accumulating wealth so much as a bad and impotent system of government."

The Communist Party of China and the Kuomintang of China then began facing the threat of the Japanese, who had begun attacking China in 1931. During this time, the Communist Party of China began to expand its influence and recruitment from within the Kuomintang of China. Chiang felt that in order to repel the Japanese, the struggle between the Communist Party and the Kuomintang needed to end first. The struggle between the two political parties continued throughout the Second World War, with both sides fighting the Japanese as they saw fit.

Following the end of the Second World War, war continued between the two parties. By 1949, the Kuomintang of China had retreated to Taiwan, and the Communist Party of China was established in mainland China. For a short time, Guangzhou had served as the capital of the Republic of China, forcing many of residents of the city to flee to British Hong Kong. During the initial takeover, many of the buildings and monuments that the Communist Party did not agree with were destroyed, prompting a period of new construction.

The words of Smith regarding the economy of Guangzhou seemingly came true under the Communist Party, as the region saw little in way of economic development. It was not until after the death of Chairman Mao Zedong, the key founder of the People's Republic of China, in 1976, that Guangzhou began to prosper economically. The heavily populated city once again opened itself up to foreign markets and trade, allowing it to become one of the most economically prosperous cities in China, with a gross domestic product of around $248 billion.

Mao

Although much has changed in Guangzhou since the First Opium War with Britain, the struggle with illegal drugs continues in the city. The American government has offered assistance in stopping drug trafficking in Guangzhou by establishing an office for the United States' Drug Enforcement Administration (DEA), but American motives in helping the Chinese get rid of the opioid problem that has plagued them for more than a century are not exactly altruistic. In reality, the Americans are attempting to combat the opioid crisis back home, as the DEA believes that China, and Guangzhou in particular, is a major source for synthetic opioids. This assessment has been argued against by the Chinese government, even as China continues receiving help from the DEA (AP 06 January 2017).

Online Resources

Other books about Chinese history by Charles River Editors

Bibliography

Associated Press. 06 January 2017. DEA Opens Shop in China to Help Fight Synthetic Drug Trade. VOA News. *https://www.voanews.com/a/dea-opens-shop-in-china-to-help-fight-synthetic-drug-trade/3666826.html* Accessed 07 March 2017

Bretschneider, E. 1871. *On the Knowledge Possessed by the Ancient Chinese of the Arabs and Arabian Colonies and Other Western Countries, Mentioned in Chinese Books.* London: Trübner & Co.

British Parliamentary Papers. 1840. XXXVI. Quoted in: Jay, John. 2010. *China: The First Opium War.* New York: University of New York.

Brinkley, Captain F. 1904. *China: Its History Arts and Literature vol. X.* London: T.C. & E.C. Jack

Cheng, Andrew; Geng, Xiao. 6 April 2017. Unlocking the potential of Chinese cities. *China Daily.*

Chin, James K. 2004. Ports, Merchants, Chieftans and Eunuchs: Reading Maritime Commerce of Early Guangdong. In: Müller, Shing; Höllmann, Thomas O.; Gui, Putao, Gui. (eds.) 2004. *Archäologie und frühe Texte.* Wiesbaden: Harrassowitz Verlag

Elleman, Bruce A. 2001. *Modern Chinese Warfare, 1795-1989.* London: Routledge

Fay, Peter Ward. 1975. *The Opium War: 1840-1842.* North Carolina: University of North Carolina Press

Guangzhou Population 2018. *http://worldpopulationreview.com/world-cities/guangzhou-population/* Accessed 6 March 2018.

Halsall, Paul. 2000. *East Asian History Sourcebook: Chinese Accounts of Rome, Byzantium and the Middle East, c. 91 B.C.E. – 1643 C.E.* Fordham University.

Jin, Yijiu. 1933. *Islam.* Boston: Brill

Lewis, Mark Edward. 2009. *China's Cosmopolitan Empire: The Tang Dynasty.* Cambridge: Belknap Press

MacPherson, Duncan. 1842. *Two Years in China: Narrative of the Chinese Expedition, from Its Formation in April, 1840, till April, 1842.* London: Saunders and Otley

Merriam-Webster's Collegiate Dictionary, 11th ed. *Cantonese.* Springfield: Merriam-Webster

Michie, Alexander. 1900. *The Englishman in China vol. I*. London: William Blackwood and Sons

Müller, Shing; Höllmann, Thomas O.; Gui, Putao, Gui. (eds.) 2004. *Archäologie und frühe Texte*. Wiesbaden: Harrassowitz Verlag

Platt, Stephen R. 2012. *Autumn in the Heavenly Kingdom: China, the West, and the Epic Story of the Taiping Civil War*. New York: Alfred A. Knopf

Roberts, J.A.G. 1999. *A Concise History of China*. Cambridge: Harvard University Press

Short, John R. 1992. *Human Settlement*. Oxford: Oxford University Press, p. 212

Smith, C.A. Middleton. 1920. *The British in China and Far Eastern Trade*. London: Constable & Co. Ltd.

Tao, Hu. 2016-02-02. Ancient shipwreck unlocks secrets of Maritime Silk Road. *Xinhua http://www.xinhuanet.com/english/2016-02/02/c_135068362.htm*. Accessed: 08 March 2018.

Twitchett, Denis; Loewe, Michael, eds. 2008. The Former Han Dynasty. In: *The Cambridge History of China: Volume 1: The Ch'in and Han Empires, 221 B.C.–A.D. 220*. Cambridge: Cambridge University Press.

Walker, Hugh Dyson. 2012. *East Asia: A New History*. Indiana: AuthorHouse

Free Books by Charles River Editors

We have brand new titles available for free most days of the week. To see which of our titles are currently free, click on this link.

Discounted Books by Charles River Editors

We have titles at a discount price of just 99 cents everyday. To see which of our titles are currently 99 cents, click on this link.

Printed in Great Britain
by Amazon

47560428R00031